Rain and Embers

To Chelsea —
May 2020 bring you happiness!

Rain and
Embers

Ali Nuri

ali-nuri.com

LCCN: 2019911021
ISBN 978-0-578-55554-6
Ebook ISBN 978-0-578-55149-4
Hardcover ISBN 978-0-578-55900-1

Printed in the United States of America
10 9 8 7 6 5 4 3 2 1

Edited by Elizabeth Catura
Book Design by Emir Orucevic

For Jeffar

autism does not define you
nor do mute reflections
render you speechless

you spoke in smiles,
the only words
worth hearing

Contents

كُنْ كَالزَّهرة

التي تُعطي عِطرَها ،

حتّى لليَد التي تَسحقُها

—الإمام علي بن أبّي طالب

be like a flower
that gifts its fragrance
to the hand that crushes it

Imam Ali Ibn Abi Talib

To Be a Murmur

I hid my voice
it sounded wrong
the way it said my name

I hid my voice
they said not to speak
in the native tongue of my mother

I hid my voice
not all tyranny
is the same

I hid my voice
they told me not to say such lies
that the Holocaust had long since gone
that they've learned much since then

I hid my voice
it gave life to atrocities
in distant lands—
in camps torched to ash

I hid my voice
it only sang of sorrow
and sadness had no place

I hid my voice
it dared to make me human
if they had only wanted to listen

I hid my voice
but I haven't forgotten how to move my mouth
to form the words that weigh heavily on my chest

The Undesirables

نور الف شمس

بِسْمِ اللهِ الرَّحْمٰنِ الرَّحِيْمِ

ربي ارحمني لأنهم لا يرحمون

though my lips are dry,
the taste of alcohol still lingers

forgive me, ancestors
for I had thought them waters of divinity—
gods and deliverance found in the bottom of bottles
but I'm still sober with horror

please grant me the serenity
to begin on the right side
of where I had been left

born to shifting sands,
I am a flower without roots
learning to bloom in the wind
carried across sun-kissed deserts,
a king exiled from paradise

I wore my father's sins
how dare he stand as a pacifist
without a choice
rising to fight against
Saddam's tyranny,
evil's ugly face

though the Iraqi Shi'a lost three revolutions
time couldn't age them, restless they never became
fear couldn't silence what pride couldn't tame
though it coursed through their veins

lions without a kingdom
nomads without a home
Roma reborn—

riches to rags
to stitched-together tents
made of trash

the wealth of refugees
can't be measured
in what was left to burn
in unholy flames—
towers of Babel
scorched Babylon

but napalm couldn't torch
a righteous wisdom
passed through the centuries
lingering inside unwavering DNA—
the swelling voice of Imam Hussain

Shi'a refusing to bury belief,
to find solace in safety,
to drown salvation
in unjustified peace

our ancestors
from nearly 1400 years ago
marched from the ancient past
to stand by our side, not to fight a hopeless war
but to continue a struggle against hate

monsters masquerading as kin
demons preaching torture—
the mutilation of innocence
in hands not meant to hold
anything

except for a plea
asking for redemption,
humanity's absolution

Cultural Chimera

I have two names
speak two languages

a refugee
of two places

struggling with being
the wrong ethnicity
twice over—

in the eyes of my roots
and where I am asked
to bury them

torn
between east and west
sun and moon

an eclipse
that doesn't get to witness
the magic of its being

resisting against the image
of supposed impossibility,
delaying its birth furthermore

the unity of two
without conflict

an omen
that even in darkness
miracles are born

Scorched Earth

I found your redemption
in the love you have for her
your daughter,
my sister

half my blood
but the whole of me

and yet I never forgot the red glow,
the way you made grey metal
burn bright with anger,
the way it seared my skin—
the incineration of my innocence

no, I never forgot the pain
felt in the short seven years
leading up to then—
still feel somehow
nearly three decades in

I'm sorry—
I want to try
and remember
only your smile

to keep only
your faith in me
and bear witness
to the father you are
in her eyes

The Devil's Music

in eyes,
I saw how an iris
comes to resemble a nebula

the patterns like sonnets—
a universe from darkness,
shadows into life

the color of green
when only ever witnessed
were blues

Wisdom

green grass
as vast as a blue sea

yet 'neath the soil
the stench of decomposition
reeks

the color stained
a dirty brown

maggots, worms, and centipedes—
a thousand ghoulish creatures
gorging themselves
on dead flesh

the withered and discarded
remnants of a life
that only ate
light

Sumerian Wings

eyes rise and fall,
bidding farewell
to forgotten ruins—
an almost towering city
now resting only in memories
yet somehow still perched
between two rivers

Babylon offended ancient Mesopotamian gods
upon reaching to repaint a moonlit indigo sky
wishing to dress the heavens with beautiful vivid petals—
fragile flowers meant to be worn as colorful dresses
hanging elegantly on the curves
of fiery, radiant, naked stars

newfound Eden withered away
becoming lost to time

twice now
humanity has been exiled
from promised paradise,
a third when a refugee fled the garden
attempting to escape a serpent
clothed in the skin of a tyrant

a reflection peers
from within salted waters—
reminiscence of home

a Tigris leaps
on another beast
branded Euphrates
they still run
on a yellow
wasteland

my desert-colored skin

Eve and Her Mother

beautiful
childless
desert

and a flower is born

humanity, too, follows suit
a silent womb no more

birthed from
her or him
earth or god

no matter the architect
be it mother or father—

the womb
should have been
a tomb

she is much older now,
older than her age
he dies a myth,
an absent father

watch them wither away

into dirt
into dust
into sand

Ode to Your Wings

dear you,
flying out of sight,
too close to the sun,
you who did not burn

orchestra in remorse—
the song of a butterfly
between two fragile wings

I hope that when we fade
our secrets stay with us,
stay with us in the grave
hidden away beneath the dirt,
beneath our lungs, buried deep
within the earth

let time make them ancient,
let them rot with the passing of years
for the truth is not meant to be shared—

people will always be strangers
even if we've made them a home
within our souls

I'm afraid of waking up
to a world where you see
and I am not what you saw

Fantasia

I close my eyes
and the dream
begins anew

they're all there too
every human soul
just as they were before

yet even in this place
beyond the reach of time
beyond the scope of space

they remain broken
tiny voices in the dark
shadows in the light

symphonies
without an audience
a stage, a sound

Ouroboros

I seek simplicity—
hungry for creativity,
just asking for a little originality
such a cliché age
recycled lines
       repeated phrases
            reiterated existences
I've become a half-starved writer,
a gluttonous man of letters,
devouring every poet
trying to feed an
insatiable hunger

craving adventure
yet can't afford
to move an inch

somebody free my mind
from these unanswerable questions
help me discover the echoes
hidden in the oceans

whale songs containing lyrics of wisdom—
sea turtles swimming to familiar shores,
burying their eggs in the very beaches
where they first stumbled into life

silver-scaled salmon
navigating upstream,
rushing to fertilize the waters
that had spawned them

elephants returning
to mourn their dead
in graveyards made
of giant bones

Cartography

there is this poem
I've been meaning to write
though it isn't about love
but maybe, just maybe
it could have been

faith isn't enough
to create a foundation
for temples to be built upon

brick doesn't form
in the breath
of wants and desires

and like the lines
we draw on a map

to say
who we are
what we are
where we come from

they are as meaningless
as the colors of our skin
the shapes of our hands
the sounds of our voices

Dualities in Clay

I thought I saw magic come alive
I thought life was just a breath
someone exhales

and that it manifests itself
in the perception of a lover

a beautiful moment
is followed by many more
until sadness overcomes it,
then it too is followed
by many more

it is a cycle of joy and sorrow,
never really one or the other,
just a bit of both

there is only one instance
repeating itself—the same story
told in multiple ways,
yet the foundation
remains the same

as if it would crumble
if it were any different

Dead Matter

the futility of glimmering cities,
neon, steel, and concrete standing tall—
the lights of our sins

they shine
oh, they shine
blissfully, defiantly

eternally
      (if only)

but the lie was spoken,
a promise made yet broken

faded—
struggling to breathe
on the very breath
that gave it life,
that gave birth
to its embers

they burn
oh, they burn
dimly, briefly

tragically
      (if only)

murmurs are all that remain,
empty pleas hurling through the abyss
abortions of monuments that never were

they are but whispers—
the darkness of our deeds

Visions of Eminence

Sahara *sinfonietta*,
a symphony in the sand
devastation howling to the air
wishing to be whole again,
a desert orchestra
in perfect unison

a yellow sea
blowing in the wind
and yet it remains only emptiness—
mirages glistening in the distance,
a monotheistic nostalgia
barely remembered

each speck of dust
desiring to be the peak,
dreaming to be insurmountable
the dunes form—an image reflecting greatness
singing songs of hope, chanting *almost Everest*

yet the pile stands trembling
beneath the weight of the wind,
sensitive to the softest touch

even a kiss from the breeze
fragments the fragile peace

Sierra's sorrow
unable to mount a ton of ache
into a foundation for the sky
to ever rest upon

it is what it is—
a formless, fractured
wasteland existence

White Shroud

napalm dropped but I was saved
to witness a different type of fire
my dad
      my hero
            my inspiration
an engineer without equal
a brilliance that devoured philosophies
and spit them back out as newfound religion

my father spared my eyes from Saddam's sins
so I could experience real horror,
torture in the hands of my parent
searing my skin at the age of seven

I found his redemption—
why can't I find mine?

went searching for salvation,
found my savior in senseless drunkenness
I confessed my sins between the slurs
trying to find a way to make sense
of being born with too much skin
I don't remember much,
except holding onto faith's hand—
a grip that had recently cleansed me
a prophet working miracles

my dad
made grey metal
turn a bright angry red
the color matching his scalding gaze—
both mirroring the trembling blood in my veins

even as it boiled,
searing my skin
making of ugly
an uglier thing

months later,
I learned to smile at him again
I knew love, still knew love,
even as he led me into a room
where holy men dressed in white
pretended to be healers

I moved religiously,
wanting to please them
I did as they pointed,
instructing me where to be
inside the massive room
containing only a single bed—
a gurney intended for the dead

I was stiff, the image of winter,
frozen by its cold embrace
yet it was nothing compared to theirs—
the worst kind of cruelty shaped in silence

before I could part my lips
to protest against a lack of consent

their arms and hands
pinned my malnourished body
to what should have been my resting place

ever since then
my memory fades to white noise
the only sounds I can recall
are my inner screams ringing loudly
the echoes traveling through time,
gripping me with terror,
and I feel it happening
all over again

my *dishdasha* being pulled over my face,

the thin cotton shrouding me in silence,
an attempt at mercy for my untainted sight
to cover the mutilation of my genitals—
maybe to hide the pain from their eyes,
the terror in my gaze as they sheared
my dignity, my innocence, cutting off
a piece of my flesh meant to be discarded—

such a waste of skin,
unclean trash
according to their God

Pantone 448 C

I am a beast without beauty
no flower can flourish in desert sands
there's no castle to be made from ragged tents

born with
the wrong name,
to the wrong race
in the wrong place

a ~~prisoner~~ *refugee* placed
in Saudi concentration camps—
money branded it with a pretty name,
something synonymous with refuge

its reality a waking nightmare

the world simply got bored
pretending to care
for that brief
four year
second

Hide and Seek

standing here wondering
if I'm mad, deaf, or blind
reflecting on the one truth—
my flesh reduced to ash
in the hands of my parents

my father swore it was love
as he beat the fear of God out of me
but I grew older and found him again,
my liquid salvation—God making ghosts
of distant memories, until all that remains
are wisps of dusk refusing to fade
from drunken bliss into dawn

I wake to flames,
my mother set ablaze
as she ties her son in ropes
condemning him to rot in the closet

but I learned to have faith back then,
when doors opened and ropes
fell near my feet

she would smile
as if remembering her humanity,
whispering for me to forget the horror
of the day that had just occurred
and only now beginning
as my father returned home
to a house made of bones

The Mirage of a Forest in the Ruins

I was born to shifting sands,
not to dreams of dirt—
the seeds of my being
never knew what flowers
would come to bloom

uprooted,
but only in thought
never lingering in a place long enough
for roots to bury themselves into a land
that may come to resemble home

torn between east and west
learning to walk crookedly—
a nomad not by choice
of one's own steps
yet hoping it reflected
at least a notion of elegance

I became antique with time,
a sundial that never knew its purpose—
only the *cold shadows* cast by parts obstructing the light
it wanted so desperately to embrace
so that it may come to know
the comfort of warmth

torn between past and present
I am neither sun nor moon
never able to become
the whole of one day

Ballerina—

a lone dancer
yearning, beckoning
once more to be with others
family, friend, or lover

yet to realize you enter
and leave, remaining alone
isolated even in their presence—
the experience of countless souls

you dance in the light
of all these stars
wishing to be
just as radiant

not knowing that you are the very sun
giving life to rock floating in infinite space
giving birth to the seas with your fire

what a miracle you are,
speaking an ancient language—
a thousand soundless words
uttered all at once

creating from desolation
endless eternities

Blue Doors of Elysium

in the fading winter light
clouds sail near a mountain's peak
never making it to the heavens

there's a promise of rain
yet not a single drop falls

and the furtive sun shifts,
stealing glances where it can,
placing gentle kisses
on every cliff in sight
they burn bright,
flush from the sensation

a piano
echoes in the distance
the music dances,
slowly drifting
toward the ears of eternity,
pursuing the very sounds
that created it

the scene comes together, a mosaic of sorts
a reminder to embrace the shapes of peace,
a silhouette of serenity found in overcast skies
slightly golden from the rays of the sun,
clouds reaching, wishing to touch the heavens,
a promise of rain that never comes,
eyes fixed on red-faced canyons

Say it Slowly

I've lived a life rich and full
yet it was away from you
I found pieces of my voice
in places where they didn't belong

words formed in eyes
like sunsets and rises
they lulled me to sleep
and sang me into life
every morning

eyes reflecting ocean blue,
beautiful and deep
I sank into them willingly,
passionately submerged
in their wisdom,
in their majesty

I swam to shore many times
and landed in the embrace
of sweetness and warmth,
eyes resembling the promise of autumn—
quiet and noble, with a sad serenity
forever hinted in their gaze
I fell for them, fall even now

I've known them,
their eyes like libraries—
doorways into other lives,
eyes that were never yours

yet your silhouette always lingered
a shadow slightly out of sight—
a hushed prayer to remember
the first time I saw green,
the way it pierced my soul

Between the Chambers of Dyslexia and Dyspraxia

I never learned to spell,
tripping on the curve
of every letter

I turn between the pages,
refusing to sink into secrets—
becoming someone else's spine

yet I am still torn between the two
lost behind a thousand different mirrors
reflecting faces that aren't truly mine—
trapped in double meanings,
shimmering, promising
every word will become
a breath of life

was I meant to exist like God,
a symphony without sound,
speaking only in glances or soft sighs?

my dark onyx eyes,
a mirage of almost-opals,
reflect only absence and not the heaviness of colors
I soak in their waters, arching with the weight,
trying to shape myself into iridescence,
a doorway beautiful enough
to walk through

Dead Language

brevity isn't beautiful
a rotten visage written
not to be forgotten
in places promising
to remember
nothing

threatening
to make a ghost
of me

I fear the isolation
in our race to silence,
the illusions of telepathy—
no one's meant to read a mind

we're just strangers
trying to make sense
of our own confused faces

people pretending to be
anything other
than human

Arabian Ink

may the dark rivers rise
and flow toward better days

I've got words
residing inside me
freely meandering
reshaping a wasteland
into the prospect
of treasured home again

though you've taken my worth,
trying to create desolation from value,
desert sands don't define me

there are pools
of black liquid gold
beneath the surface

so when the last winds blow,
let my meaningless yellow sea
fly away with the breeze

Rain and Embers

in the place where my heart was meant to be
rests only scorched distant memories

I remember the first time I saw rain
napalm poured from cloud-shaped planes
it flooded unpaved dirty streets
and made embers of our home

torching refuge into ash
making of refugees
nomads once again

بِسْمِ اللهِ الرَّحْمٰنِ الرَّحِيْمِ

preach of *giving*

as if it's a *sacrifice*

gifting back what was stolen

(dare to trust in *truth?* the shade of *sins* already forgiven?*)*

to move toward *faith*

yet stand witness,

gazing as *martyrs* pause,

lingering on an ancient question

what color is God?

Giver of Divinity

on the brink of despair
there is a certain kind of sadness
that resonates throughout,
stirring a being gently into existence
spawning the eternal child

born blind
yet wishing to see
so he chanted *be*
as he was conceived

giving birth as he was born,
his mind moves an everlasting pen
and every word becomes a breath of life

it's entrancing,
it is disenchanting
writing of sorrow and joy
life and
death

creating entire systems
of stars and dreams
hopes and fears

such fragile words, he weeps,
such delicate scenes...

and in the soil
of his being,
a soul is planted
bearing the fruits
of his masterpiece

from a single stem,
a garden blooms

he begins to plead
with those who have yet to see,
I've watched you awaken to countless suns,
to half-forgotten memories heavy and grey with age
and a voice not so different from his own
replies arrogantly, *one is just a man*
dreaming to be a god

despite the wisdom
that came with age,
he had more to learn

but the fruit
                falls—
a tombstone to Socrates' tree

Rot

a madness of decay
waging war inside skin and bones
waging war between flesh and ghost

it is the promise of warmth
or at least the silhouette of a house,
one that could have been called home

it is a hollow husk
moving from
town to town
moment to moment

it lingers long after it's gone, living on
in the remnants it leaves behind
in the memories of happiness
in the shadows of sadness

it is a walking edifice
that finds comfort in ruin
in the fragments of sorrow

it finds solace in the songs
playing between
the first sigh of death
and the last deep breath of life

Holy Waters

I've been singing songs inside my head
but when I speak the words fall dead
my lips have become an open coffin
may the lyrics rest in peace

I close my mouth
yet two curtains lift

midnight
       starless
               irises
glances
      gazes
             stares of emptiness

blinking visions into yesterday
time ticks, performing a ritual
summoning creatures
from a deep abyss

memories wake to haunt
a house made of bones
poltergeists live in every wall
knocking from the inside
of a frightened home
yet not a single ghost
seeks to be free
exorcism remains
but a distant remedy

Gravity

dear almost-love
attracted to darkness,
to sorrow reflected in black irises

oh, sweet incandescent sun,
emitting light to all you touch
breathing life through a kiss of fire

I am an event horizon
a heaviness not meant to be radiant
eating stars as they come to orbit my being

Man-Eater in the Mirror

you are the only lion here—

a lie and a beast
tearing into humanity,
a killer without mercy

I hope your paintings
contain the devil's colors
you willingly soak in their blood,
a conceived cruelty—a monster birthed
inside a cold, corrupted, empty chest

you're not a sapling, let alone a seed;
you're a salt grain trying to bloom
into a fucking fragile flower

Namesake

oh, beautiful reflection
a purity complete upon inception

eyes darker than night—
event horizons breathing in endless light
holding a broken universe together
stitching torn nebulas
that dared to reach
forever

born to the desert
dressed in sun-kissed skin—
~~tan~~ golden
             man
                 of sand
trapped in an hourglass
I am dash—ing to the end
falling with the times
quick(sand-
               -man) sleep no more
        wake, witness realities
borne of impossible dreams

my father,
my mother
had crowned me
towering nobility,
a lion meant to rule
all seven heavens

though my voice never spoke ill
nor ugliness to another soul
~~kneel before majesty~~

my tongue moves
speaking different languages
to explain relentless hurt—

a mercy discovered from friction,
from thought to paper

it sets the words and sins ablaze
wailing loudly, flailing in pain
they dig into me, pleading with
an unmerciful flame

The Father of Dust

بِسْمِ اللهِ الرَّحْمٰنِ الرَّحِيْمِ

لَا إِلٰهَ إِلَّا اَللهُ مُحَمَّدٌ رَسُولُ اَللهِ

وَعَلِيٌّ وَلِيُّ اللهِ
branded
with the name
of a formless god
exalted and humble
in every inhaled moment
time ticks but my essence
does not wither—
truth does not age

Alpha and Omega
I am Ali ibn Abi Talib,
the exhaled breath of divinity—
a mercy to the entirety of existence
a gateway into enlightened purpose
a voice of hopeful justice

I have journeyed the seven heavens
each a universe the size of a grain of sand
contained within the next one

I have traveled through countless dimensions,
not for selfish boisterous adventures but to entangle
with the roots of true and pure philosophy
so that I may share their seeds of wisdom,
a gift to our reality

may they flourish into a forest
of infinite limitless knowledge
a monotheistic language
weaved through an alphabet
of eloquent and refined letters
contained within all particles—
matter stitched harmoniously
into a single beautiful story

every atom
is an Adam

life isn't meant
only for humanity
but we are here to witness
the visions of majesty
in our earthly form

images seen
without the gaze
of two delicate irises

sights observed
by a presence
that rests inside
every human
chest

Descendants of Ali

despite our divine blood,
we are either cursed or blessed
only through our own actions

Layla,
we are both the lion's kin
reduced to mere cats
purring, playing house,
crafting furniture
from poetry

but the words are rigid
without any poetic respite

brief flashes of refuge
hinted in another's onyx eyes

vibrations promising to fade
earthquakes last mere seconds
but desolate entire cities into ruin
countless decades couldn't unearth
the devastation

regardless of the strength of our structure,
nothing is able to withstand the fault line
we both seem to be resting upon

Forced Pilgrimage

we are nomads
home remains
elsewhere

as foreign
as the lands we left

and the ones
we now dwell on

Salt Garden

a seed is tossed in the wind
the most beautiful flower
yet to bloom

but I should have waited
been a bit more patient
and realized I am a desert
a cruel desolate wasteland
in human form

every seed is wasted in my skin

Icy Puzzles

eye sea waves crashing
into shore lanes still reeling
from previous tsunamis' devastation

oceans of hurt—
purity salted by bitterness
poured into an open wound

rising with passion
reaching for the sun
wishing to shine just as radiantly
unable to touch its would-be parent

an ache remains, an almost formless stream of sighs—
sorrow in the shape of clouds floating as boundless memories
of what could have been a beautiful incandescent unification

the fragmented skies cry in lonely isolation
a voice thunders, a spirit tries to ignite life
but it only flashes as streaks of white light
smiting aimlessly

eyesight blurred
a million drops
falling helplessly
toward the earth
no hands, no arms
to embrace each other
one last time

regardless of the city, country
or unnamed place they land,
they fall alone

The Void and its Siren

here's to all
my broken dreams,
my hopes and fears,
the names I know,
the ones I call my own,
to all the lives I've lived
and have yet to live

here's to all
the wisdom I seek and ignore,
to the noises inside my soul,
to all the nightmares
that define my core

here's to the beauty of madness,
the music of sadness,
the silence between
the sounds

here's to the echoes of happiness,
the vibrations of the things left behind,
traveling through the valleys,
the canyons of my mind

here's to the
comforts of lies,
to the wonders of truths,
the realities too ugly to be painted
any other way

here's to its call—
the void that we can't ignore,
the one that birthed us into endless light

here's to life in the dead of night,
to the siren of existence

Minerva

an image of impossibility
—witnessing Beethoven
and the sight is madness

without voice
yet there's still songs in silence

without day
yet there's still a moonlight sonnet

you are the vibrations,
a piano's tune—
poetry written in sheet music,
sonnets into sonatas

a symphony
in the stillness
of gazing at the stars

now each question mark
resembles half a heart
and the two halves
come together—

an answer
to all life's
mysteries

(req·ui·em)

linger
      awhile
           longer

dwell inside her chest
breathe when she inhales
sigh when she exhales

I heave heavy with worry
even over gasps of air,
visiting her like a lover
who can't get enough
of her essence

oxygen speaks her name
my mantra, my tiny
newfound wisdom

a soft breeze that dances
to songs she only knows how to hum
never brave enough to sing aloud
please be merciful, oh sweet wind,
carry the hurt away with her breaths

she is courage, not just courageous—
speaking kindness through glances
walking to aid another's presence
sympathy for someone else's aches
she reaches with fragile arms
eager to embrace the broken

vibrations in grief
a symphony in agony,
her gentle heart shattering,
voice cracking—breaking,
each word fragmenting—
splintering

into countless haunting notes of sorrow
she weeps, painting the sounds of pain
sun and moon witness her sadness
both rise higher with each new day
wanting to eclipse her worries
every single night

dawn and dusk cascade,
promising endless second chances
for her to be a messiah,
a soloist cradling the entirety of darkness,
and she gladly arches with the weight
investing the whole of her being
to lift the burdens of others
onto her tender shoulders

Inspiration

your mind
carves brilliance
from invisible
breaths of air

I have no words
just chills,
shivers

spine-shaking
sensations

if I'm a sea of wonder,
you're the ocean
that birthed
my waves

Icarian Sea

dawn kisses
with the promise
endless sightings of you

you were a stranger
who rose as a thousand faces
of the ocean

the ripples you caused—
tsunamis devastating
every shore

I Only Found Three-Leaf Clovers

watching the seconds pass by
listening to the gentle drops of rain
I love how the sounds play inside my head
a soft melody, a sad song
the tune repeating
over and over

I lie awake,
drawing your name
on the ceiling
using nothing more
than the tip of my finger
and imaginary ink,
painting countless pictures,
images only I can see

this bed feels so cold, so empty
I miss your warmth, the comfort of your touch
I can't stop whispering, can't stop talking to myself

let me go, I beg you, let me be

hundreds of thoughts rush through my mind
endless rivers, streams of memories

I feel like a ghost, do I even exist to you?

I toss and turn from side to side,
trying to rid myself of the thoughts
trying to get rid of what once was

let me go, I beg you, let me be

I just want to
run in the fields
swim in the sea
float with the clouds

but my legs are so tired
and my lungs are exhausted
just trying to breathe

my arms are too short
to grab hold of the sky
and pull myself away

Cradling Stress

I am heavier today
carrying the sighs
of two people

pregnant with worry
a genderless child

given name *Anxious*
middle name *Jitters*
last name *Nervous*

my waters break
but the unborn
refuses birth

left holding
only aches

salted streams
wrinkle my skin

I'm aging
the seconds tick slowly
each breath lasting an hour

Casket of the Damned

drowning myself in liquor
trying to forget my sins
suffocating on truths
of an unbearable past

God forever missing
while Satan tempts me,
seducing me
one dance is all she asks

here's one shot for my sorrows
two shots for my pain
three shots and it's numbing
four and I'm becoming insane

five to the memories
lingering inside my brain

six, seven, eight
yet I still can't seem
to escape

nine to a man with tears
that have yet to stream
down his face

ten, eleven, twelve
yet sleep never comes
no rest for the wicked
I dance with the devil
tonight

Log # 435

I am a puzzle
puzzling over pieces
every color of man
woman and child
all desiring peace

oh, how we kid ourselves—
drugs are bad—
white lies, a shrugged reply,
they're alright

we become
the spitting image of God
coughing phlegm
our version of morality

quick to judge,
but us?
we are outside the scale
of introspection

purely due to our own choices,
choosing to cradle cruelty
becomes rather easy

there's no harm in it,
said with a wink
and an innocent smile

every sin
is weighted equally
all misdeeds are heavy
because of the desolation
they cause in others

Crusade

I saw faith shatter entire civilizations
a multitude of mighty nations
not just women and men
stuck in lonely isolation

my tears
became poetry,
emotions became words
the more broken the hurt,
the more sensual the curves

Linear

dusk to dawn
until dusk returns
once more

time
is always
breathing

inhaling sand
and exhaling dust

gods and myths
will become one
none shall remain
both buried within
the hourglass

Stubborn

the weight of every drop
falling from my shower
rewrites my thoughts,
or rather unravels them

water purified by a city
sprawling in the Mojave,
a flower that doesn't understand
it's scorched Earth and still on fire,
too hot for life to bloom

yet here sin and sun both exist
and the pilgrims of hurt
find their way too

millions seeking redemption
through a multitude
of different salvations

a shirtless holy man carries a sign,
big bold letters asking the broken
to find their way to God

and the whore dressed as a nun
sitting nearby in some nameless bar
slowly sips her wine,
savoring the taste
of intoxication

the divine liquid courage
pumps through her veins
and she rises with the beat,
lifts her drink and proclaims,

here he is

Sin City Pilgrimage

in this place where I chose to live,
beauty is a reality visible on the outside
because someone somehow knew
ideals are beautiful but for most
there's nothing pretty on the inside

Mecca in the desert
Tibet in the mountains
Paradise in the skies
truths in isolation

places meant to be sought
built in unforgiving,
unrepenting,
merciless
locations

yet the masses flock,
lost seeking to be found

smiles form only to fade again—
those who find their gods
leave them behind

after all
what happens in Vegas

s
t
a
y
s

or did everyone forget?

Metrophobia

fuck poetry
I write reality,
a language created
through an alphabet of hurt,
suffering in stark black lines—
a calligraphy of emotions,
every letter an ocean

tick, tick, tick
the minutes pass by,
aches now existing
in two different places

resting on paper
and pumping through
my tainted veins

madness or magic?
only God knows
after all, he created
this shit existence

pain remains crystal clear
yet hope is lost in mistranslations

due to a lack of communication,
the world's best-selling author
has been eerily silent
likely dying, dead,
or simply doesn't
give a damn

Deceitful Visions

there's a stench in the air
and I can't help but catch a whiff—

an untruthful person
rotting on the inside
with a bright beautiful
smile

breath reeking
of maggots feasting
on a dead tainted
purity

Treachery Through Time

et tu

Judas
      Brutus
            or Cain

anguish
      hurt
            or pain

which title to crown the head
already cursed with a silver tongue,
a person senselessly thrusting their trust
back into my spine?

maybe a rock would sit best
on such a thick-headed skull

White Noise

can't quite fade away
her figure, her frame, her shape

she looked to the skies
searching for a sign—
a shimmer of some star,
a sun that might harbor
something resembling life

she knelt in prostration—
at least it's a similar image
yet she sought to be worshiped
through some twisted truth of love,
one she could only know as messiah and creator

she was on her knees,
the white of her eyes
reflecting anything
other than a deity

her lips mirrored
the black holes of his gaze,
event horizons taking in all they taste

she took more than expected
yet didn't stop her euphoric chanting,
her head rocking as if in divine worship

she came seeking adulation,
an apotheosis through another
something to spark existence
into the empty of her being

into two irises
where her eyes
should have been

Necropolis of the Sun

[what weighs so heavy—
—to keep them from piercing into others)

i. Black Holes
event horizons are beautiful
because of their distance,
yet close enough to announce
their existence—
great reapers in the dead of night
hidden in the center of every galaxy

ii. Daughters of the Sun
I now know why we wish upon shooting stars,
anything that can come to be free of that gravity—
that *abyssal eldritch*—must be able to satiate desires
like *jinn* borne of smokeless fire

iii. Signs
and just as the eclipses seen in the skies
have come to affirm that magic is real,
these falling stars are also an omen of some *great other*—
a prophecy made eons ago, during the long night,
before time became so linear

the *singularity* bends time and space
promising to swallow reality

iv. Circular Beginnings
(my eyes grew tired before I ever
awoke into this world—

—they do not give, only take
great reapers in the dead of night]

Nearing Nirvana

despite destruction,
salvation, solace, serenity
rain ritualistically

spirits sway, surrendering
acceptance arrives
and anxiety's atoms
arise as air

wisdom's waters
wash away withered weight
worries wander
far away

farewell
forsaken
fires

Gratitude to Joy

I've known moments of happiness
but not the truth of it,
only where it lingers and lurks
in the mundane

a cup of tea, a flower,
a walk down a familiar lane

I don't know why it eludes me
I've gone from barefoot in desert sands
to autonomous cars in the urban jungle
from being stateless to the American dream
from ashes to heights never promised

yet here I am
and the sun is bright
and the room is bright
and her smile is bright

it should all just work
it should all eclipse a yearning
where every beauty sought and found
fades as she comes into focus,
more radiant than it all—

any flower,
any candle,
any streetlamp
along a road
leading nowhere

the only place worth being in
is with her, wherever she may be

yet it all
eludes me,
escapes me

whether I hold on tightly
or not at all

happiness—
is it just moments
relived in the mind,
in the heart, and always
accompanied by sorrow?
is it meant to be so fleeting?

happiness remains in fragments—
tastes, smells, and sounds
even when the light of it
wanes in absence

I found happiness
in smiles, and eyes,
and voices

ones that weren't mine
but I had a chance
to hold them still

May Artemisia Bloom

it takes place on any given day
with no clear indication
of when and where
or how and why—
it just happens

it's a feeling,
a slow tingling sensation
crawling up and down
it consumes, devouring
the soul, the body,
and finally, the mind

some call it an epiphany,
a small touch of wisdom
is it the reason for life—
meant for the one
touched by it?

is it a gentle melody
heard when death finally emerges
from the shadows and the heart slows,
ever aware of its fate, humming softly
of songs only the dead must know?

maybe it's a bird dancing through the clouds
and the sight shapes you into Icarus
flying across the skies

maybe it's a forest where imagination
is given the chance to come alive

maybe it's a picture
on some stranger's wall
that feels so familiar
one could almost
call it home

Tomorrow

fate does not lie
she is the messiah
of yet-to-be's—

it is but fiction

prophecies from a false prophet
masquerading to a melancholy lullaby,
the singing of hushed prayers
uttered from the lips
of the faithful arrogant
always dancing to that song,
to the dream of destiny

yet the nightmare is upon us
lingering in the promise of happiness

the rivers of sorrow
flow, swell, and flood

East and West

resentment
is it just for lack of adjustment—
a failure to compromise?

it's a battle for inches
and I don't know
where to draw the lines—
unable to give, yet taken anyway

my fears, they thrive in your tears
every drop giving birth, giving life to them—
dignity drowns in the sounds of suffering

I live to set you free—
shackled and chained,
I am tied to your feet,
clearing obstacles with my teeth,
for no god can walk on unholy ground

I am blinded by devotion,
the worship of a false idol
you are only human
and I am the metamorphosis
of infinite solutions to your every problem—

for I have only one
take my will, my pride,
yet I'll still continue
to walk your path
just to say
I'm not
alone

Ishmael's Monomania

witness a canvas breathing,
innocence exhaling *gentle sighs*,
an absence of color—*white
noise*—sounds masquerading as thoughts

stuck on repeat, humming echoes
of almost-rainbows tainted by human touch

dusk fades to dawn
darkness bathes in red light
twilight of the morning star
Lucifer's melancholia—*belief*

a tiny voice of God,
madness rejecting insanity
a single note, yet it's as if hearing
endless orchestras—rivers in the air

blues
            that won't let go
greens
            that won't come home
yellow's
            bright silent emptiness

darkness' touch
a sundial's silhouette

ticking away
            ticking away
                        ticking away

ugliness curves
words almost form
voices almost song
music almost born

stories of absence,
forgotten memories

dust peers through time,
a sandstorm blinding purity's sight
and white wails in the heart of the sea,

which is more insane,
repetition or faith
in the same old same?

indigo's unholy devotion
grasping at the shapes of love
relics from distant lands
slipping between tear-
drenched fingers

it's been weeks
and the years lived
still have yet
to exist

so this is the color of hurt
a sorrow not meant to be
painted

a pain so deep
no metaphor
could ever
describe it

Dredge

fear now shapes my breath
it's hot, it's cold, it's anything
but itself

fear now holds my tongue
my words, my mind
I am chained to hurt
to pain, to aches
I didn't think
I could withstand

yet here I am
with parts of me missing
pieces newly torn
but I still feel their shapes

an eagle with sharpened vision,
I saw the outcome of your decisions
but I forgot to look at myself

for when the dust settled,
the ruins that remained
didn't paint an image
of the beauty
that had been
desolated

Currents

creativity
is more than
just a breath

it runs through veins
a marathon without end

shaping rigid
golden mountains
from a yellow sea of sand

Misplaced Sapling

a single dead deciduous *tree* in Qurna—
a flower reflects on the image *of* a newfound parent
roots run deep near the Tigris river, *knowledge* makes branches
from withered petals trying to bloom in the shadows of sequoias

Between Roots and Ash

I never found promise
nor truth in the sound
I heard them make

the one spoken
by my father
the one whispered
by my mother

I saw a shackle
try and shape me
mold me
into an image
created by another

they saw an apparition

they gave him life
before they gave me
the chance to live

taught me
to move my tongue
and make a noise
that hurt to say

my name

Sailing to Pacify the Storm

before it blows away
your newfound home
back into formless dirt
and broken wood again

the earth won't reclaim it
despite the scorching sun

the pile refuses to rot
standing as a reminder
an effigy to love

that could have been
that could have been
that could have—

Urban Jungle

desert lion
so far away from home

roaming city streets
a nomad lost without purpose

a man-eater trying to find any flower
with even a few drops of dew
to quench your panting thirst

Racism

born the wrong color
but looking right again—
golden, golden sun-kissed
baby, you don't compare

I've got your shade
and it's merciless—
another white person
tearing into someone tan

speaking in tongues, hissing half-truths
but saying nothing worth a damn

I'm still human,
did you forget?

guess Sunday school never taught much—
you're all still flirting with devils

Not an Immigrant

how brave, they say,
to choose to leave

how they would never
abandon faith or family

it's not a choice

even now,
I don't find it easy
to get up and go—
all I ever sought was refuge,
not the promise of *home*

I swear

a flower uprooted
carried away in the breaths
of thirty-two hard, harsh,
and unforgiving a-gusts

it would seek a temporary truce,
not the promise of peace

I swear

ironic how I want to be seen
as a little more than less
and realizing just now
that I am an *it*
without a sense
of place

how have I come to know such faith
in the images painted of me by hands
other than my own?

how have I come to this,
to willingly shred—not just shed—my name,
to shout along to the deceitful truth
my heart now believes in?

how have I come to this,
this no-man's-land

where I choose
to speak of the aches,
the anger, the agony

but somehow,
they only appear
as shadows

because fear grips me
and I turn away
to be confronted by anything
but the ugliness made by man,
sometimes by my own
two hands

Almost Human

بسم الله الرحمن الرحيم

horror deforms the pure,
torture torments the soul

'til those
who once stood against evil
become demons of their own
now wearing the face of Satan
death to the ethnicity of hatred!
they didn't whisper, they chanted
stepping on ashes, an already sacrificed
burnt innocence—

who cares? he's just an Iraqi, nothing sacred

born to the wrong color, the shade of Pantone 448 C—
a hue too ugly to ever reflect the beauty of humanity
branded with a name too difficult to pronounce,
a sound unholy made through phlegm
too disgusting to utter—
who dares speak such ill,
who dares to spit out the taste of sickness,
a menacing threat in the way Arabic letters curve

impossible for a desert alphabet
to mirror the elegance of speech
their mouths won't open
their tongues refuse to move
their lips won't part to emit
a noise so foreign—عَلِيّ

Nasir

my worries fade, only his remain
but he is anger—not salvation
he will end his life, he claims
peace will be had
blood is thicker
than water

it is the murder of his soul,
no matter the flesh
he devours

hope—
a second coming
to redeem his father
but he will not embrace
a better tomorrow
even for the sake
of his unborn
daughter

...

..

.

life and death knocking on his door
Laila almost through the gates
God, please grant mercy for eyes
darker than shadows

beauty made less from the soot barely left
by the cruel arms of would-be parents
and ashes created by the brother
that couldn't
that couldn't
even now
even now
even—

I would rewrite history
  to steal away your tragedy
    though I stood as the eldest
I could not shield you from the hurt
napalm would have been mercy now
we should have perished, not suffered
death of innocence in family's hands
I tried to shoulder the weight of it
  five of you, yet the whole of me
sorrow is all I take to the grave
I couldn't protect any of you
my siblings, my tiny almost
children, I should have
been an inspiration
a way out of
darkness
I am
s
o
r
r
y

I'm Looking Up

but the pꞁɿoʍ is 'up-'side uʍop

insane lines inside the mind
of some random stranger—
this is me written down on papyrus,
Egyptian paper minus the hieroglyphics
and I live and die in these lines I write

I am asleep with both eyes wide open,
lied to myself and said I have a purpose

years of being a nobody,
chasing after shadows
trying to become somebody

feelings of insignificance near a mountain's side
tiny even when compared to a blue whale's eye
climbing trees to feel like a giant
touching the clouds
wishing I could fly

so abstract,
my own thoughts
try to escape themselves

ocean deep—
drowning inside myself,
suffocating on dry land
lost in a watery,
teary-eyed labyrinth

I tried to be more than fantasy—
opened gateways into different realities
read countless books
      until I became,
            until I became,
                  until I became

                am I nothing
            but fiction?
am I water—liquid
taking the form of life?

I live, I live
but am I even alive?

and what do you say
when your own soul
questions your sanity?

where do you go
when there is nowhere left
and you realize you've just been
chasing yourself?

unanswered questions
tick relentlessly inside
time continues to drift
the seconds inch
toward the promise
of a familiar tomorrow

Human Connection

shackled to the floor—
freedom's prisoner
I roam wide open roads
almost heading somewhere

reality isn't that strange
I see the patterns—
the world's a stage
and I'm winning
endless accolades

people used to interest me
now I only mirror the person
I speak with

I input,
you output
action, reaction
nothing deep,
nothing personal

I see them, I paint them
and they fall in love with the image—
a picture meant to be hung on my wall
but blank walls have always made
more sense to me

we're so detached from ourselves
yet we seek comfort in each other
as if a single chest could contain
two blood-pumping muscles

Isolation

peering into a sea of silhouettes
as if the sight were mere shadows
yet people are not so easily deciphered

each complex
a universe unfolding
inside them

aimless
they seem
yet aimless
they're not

immersed
in a restless cycle
of day and night
joy and sorrow
hope and despair
hurt and healing

so on
       and
             so on…

Earthly Sickness

when did innovation
suddenly become so evil?

modern medicine,
advances in chemistry,
paradise a plane ride away

the entirety of human history
and all knowledge within reach—
a few clicks and you're transported
to a different time period to learn from the past
and try to make the earth of tomorrow
a better place today

laws, equality, reconstructive surgery,
cellphones, internet, self-driving cars,
and earthquake-proof architecture

technology is good—
people with misguided intentions
are the problem

did we forget that it's *humanity*
that's causing environmental degradation?

holocausts and camps
still exist around the world
from America to China

and millions of slaves create towers of Babel,
scorching the heavens in the dunes of Abu Dhabi

as if people weren't
the very same autoimmune disease
meant to be the salvation of this planet

Obsolete Letters

a horde lies dead
blackened blood stains the dirt
darkness seeps into brown earth
disappointment slowly surfaces
and sighs replace spoken language—

blank stares
empty gazes
eyes speaking
Morse code

a man sits in solitude
blinking thoughts
into obscurity
a voice of anguish
remains unheard

were the sounds just static—
white noise and not a whispered pain?
burdens dared to be shared because another said
they could shoulder the weight of ache

but a marriage of letters
still ceases to exist—
the words won't form
and now silence falls
between them

a blanket to prevent
further miscommunication

Hush

in the stillness
the brief quiet
found in between
all the little drops of rain
drumming away on the surface
of whatever is willing to play their song

in that frozen moment
the one hidden in the chaos
of chasing serenity
there is a faded reflection
of tranquility

an aching sadness
found in between the sounds
we weren't meant to listen for

Canvas

you spoke

I fall once more into darkness
worlds ignite into being
and my essence entangles
in a familiar warmth

an ache
a longing for you
before the truth of you
is born

a clock ticks
a brush moves

you're an artist
painting with sentences
destroying the worlds
spoken into creation

Muse

this dance of you and I
is the flickering of flames
a fire raging in the dead of night

to be yours
is to be entangled
with the source of poetry

the letters shape themselves
line after line they assemble
from a fountain of ink

your love
is a mother to words
a parent to poetic purpose

but alas
what is to remain
of kindling if not ash?

Devotions

I don't know if my mouth can form the words
to describe what ghost of some god came over me

I love the way your words move
making dunes as if by design
patterns in the sand
art in retrospect

your flow gives way to rhyme
and then back again
to head in a new direction

I have only chills,
no words to offer
my tongue moves
but only my spine
curves into language

and my skin,
my hair, my whole body
wants to be free from itself

California Daydreams

you are brilliance
no amount of persistence
or resilience will ever shape another
into a vision that matches your radiance
you are the true color of iridescence

incandescent,
they want to be illuminated—
but there's only one sun in the sky
and you're that fire in human form

your aura can scorch worlds
or breathe life into them

a kiss of ash
and oceans still emerge

if you're not God
then all of divinity

is a lie

Kaity

your fiction is my truth
your fantasies my paradise
your eyes are a gateway to your soul
and I wish to float in the ocean
that is your mind

take me with you
when you dream tonight

tell me stories
show me the world
in a different light

I want to see the colors
of the rainbow in your sky

to get lost in your thoughts
and I ask you not to find me
'til I reach your heart

Chrysalis

the way every letter curves
into a new word and every word
into a new line and every line
a stroke closer to painting
the whole of you
before I come to know your color,
a splendor I don't quite understand

I breathe slowly between the pauses
between the letters that shape your name
hoping to know why love fades
from abstract philosophy
to raw naked truth

Snow White Butterfly

i.
sitting outside some nameless bar
watching other lives casually walk on by
their smiles slowly becoming mine,
their happiness a reason to embrace joy

despite the sorrow—
no matter the desolation
raging inside

ii.
a white butterfly dances erratically—
a fragile flower between two small wings
flying gracefully to kiss its rooted kin,
a sunflower dressed in brilliant petals

iii.
I drift into a stream,
my thoughts meandering
within the glistening dream

and before I fade away,
the butterfly lands on my cheek
gifting me kindness with its presence

Dawn

dear you,
my aurora in the sky,

I have words to share
of the art my eyes have
come to know intimately

but my hand will not move,
will not pen, will not curve on paper
to a language that does not capture
the contours of your being

my lips will not use
an earthly language
to make of you
faded reflections—
a caged morning bird

it would never recreate
the sounds of your melody
and I would not dare confine you,
for what beauty would remain in rainbows
without the nameless shades of your colors?

Mornings

eyes wide open
like a new day dawning
toward unexpected horizons

my sorrows lift into parted lips
I kiss, I lick the places below
her hips

she tastes like honey,
sweet and sticky
she drips heaven
on me

she tastes like the gods
had blessed the spaces
in between her legs

her mouth moves
possessed by ecstasy
oh, I hope she moans in Farsi—
it's the true language of poetry—
but the only sound that escapes
is the sweet sigh of sex
becoming love as it's exhaled

Selene

where is it you go
when you go?

those thoughts,
how far do they take you?

where is it you go
when you go?

when you stare off
into the distance

you dance
with the wind
you sway, so I pretend

I watch you fall
to a gentle breeze
singing,

I only find us
when I think of you

you are home
> *you are home*
>> *you are home to me*

Iris

your eyes,
they dance with answers
to never-ending questions

they twinkle
like no stars I've ever seen
and I must look away

for man
should not stare
in the eyes of God

and like the God you are,
I wait for you to breathe life into me
with just a single word—
sometimes not even,
when a simple look
would do

you move me in such ways
that I no longer feel my body
as my own

rather, it becomes yours
and I am happy not just to share
but to give it all, all of it to you

Regrets of a Life Not Lived

I have lived
a thousand times
with nothing but
the thought of you,
lives shared together
in different places

quiet scenes in ancient towns
where we sit to drink coffee on a park bench
becoming entranced by the dissonance of others
—the white noise of life

but I let a thought remain just that—
as prostration gives way to obeisance
and I to the apotheosis of another

The Window of Longing

he wrote as quietly
as the thoughts inside his head,
and if you ever read them,
his words, you'd swear that they
weren't written but rather whispered

some swore that they were oceans
and that you could submerge yourself in them
but you would never reach a bottom

he wrote of
love and God
reason and madness
but the words were never enough
it seemed as though he would flood the world
with his thoughts yet no ark was in sight

he doesn't write that way anymore
he writes about a future that he might not have,
about a lovely woman in a yellow sundress and a straw hat
he writes about children who smile at her,
and how she would smile back

I swear
I felt his heart singing
I heard him say,
paradise, paradise,
heaven is just a few moments away

I don't think he was speaking of death
or meeting up with God—
he was talking about another life,
a dream yet to be a reality

he cried silently,
and I don't know why
but it hurt to see him that way

Grow Ancient

time is cynicism
for a love that old
is not beautiful

it is tainted—
God ever the witness
to darkest temptation

inception is idealistic
the beginning has yet to
stain the allure

it is unadulterated—
Lucifer eternally lurking
in the shadows

Spider

suck
the life
out of me

your bright smile
a reminder of your power
your teeth bite fear into me

I come today,
tomorrow
I'll come
again

your emptiness will be full
with the essence of life

a war won
victim to myself
and your gaze

the way you spread your legs
and both pairs of your lips
a garden in motion

I'm hanging from a noose
tied around my neck

being guided in wonder
awestruck by your sensations
you speak and I can't help but listen
weave those bits of what you took
back into this hollow body

I am haunted by the image
of my missing ghost
stolen through
a consistent, constant

swallowing of my seed,
my purity, my dignity

desolated,
I lie in ruins
and you lie,
saying an ancient civilization
is reborn—fabrications

do either of us know the truth anymore
or just a twisted faith in our own versions
of something resembling honesty,
visions blind to reality?

two broken
don't make one whole—
just more holes
pieces too jagged
tearing more pockets
attempting to create
some semblance of peace
so we keep prodding in darkness
hoping emptiness might somehow cave,
collapsing from the nagging persistence
the insanity of rep·e·ti·tion stabbing
from different pointed ends

fuck madness
or one of us will need a coffin
I buried my spirit in your body
and an idea doesn't die
so that only leaves you
resting in isolated silence

alone yet I'm standing in your presence
welcome to a society lacking sanity
I kneel proclaiming another as nobility

rule over the maggots—
may your reign
be eternal

the arachnid king is dead
long live the widow queen

Waiting Between the Pauses

another familiar stranger waits at my door
trying to enter someplace that might have
resembled home

confusion mirrors frustrated rattling
another knob refusing to open
wondering where their key
had been forgotten

likely lost in dark dirty alleys
dropped off alongside sanity,
any sense of reason

a momentary dignity
faint noises, echoes
sounds almost
remembered

entering without thought,
refusing the mercy to knock
instantly freezing,
caught in a polar vortex
an unspoken, uninvited greeting
a piercing gaze forcing cold
to sink deeper than bone

a statue stands frozen in silence
pondering how to safely thaw
a frosty jaw threatening to devour—
not just bite—the last breath of life
unconvincing eyes peer in awe,
witnessing sparks from friction,
heated breath rising
loose from icy shackles,
a tango of refuting and accusing
ignites once more

how dare I twirl around their truth
to dance with shadows, a hundred other silhouettes

just lifeless imagined ghosts,
not the light of reality
—never realizing
that one of them
is theirs

I Do

sometimes the door of love is icy cold
frozen walls dressed in human clothes

vows lost meaning, meandering
in nameless arctic streams
drifting toward further isolation—
an empty tundra of dementia

memories thaw, floating near familiar rivers
humanity returning to a remembered house again
pausing, peering pensively through an open window

warm air rising to embrace the wind
with the comforting scent of sweetness
created through the cooking of different dishes
countless flavors of happiness

ingredients that included
silly songs and dance
witnessed only by
elation's blissful gaze

eyes speaking smiles
curving
            forming
                        savoring
a sight of jubilation—
aching shapes of longing

'til death...
no—these visions
will surely outlast
the afterlife

The Breath of Love—

crushing us whole with its weight
the pressure pounds insanity
into our brains

tearing to fragments
a delicate peace
hammered
into place

until the only sane thought
is sighing someone else's name
as if the syllables were the very air
we're meant to breathe

but oxygen couldn't replace
the choking suffocation
of sweetly kissed letters
if they dare depart
parted lips

carried away to far-off horizons
on the spine of a merciless breeze
never to be inhaled again

The Shape of Absence

sometimes I speak just to hear the echo
of your name being carried by the wind
to know you existed, to know you're real

I lost my voice trying to resuscitate the sound
a voice of a thousand symphonies seeking
to hear the song of summer again

the truth is
it's always been about a letter
waiting to be written

a letter to every single second
that continues to escape me

Your Air is So Familiar

you were
but a moment
far too fragile
to be anything
more

a single glance
a melody to a forever
yet to be—never to be

I remain entranced
by the life I've lived,
still to live

in that everlasting
ethereal gaze
of yours

Sophia

Greek or Persian
she remains true
to both name
and meaning
beautiful wisdom

bathed in a kiss of fire
on the day she was born
her skin golden
seeping from
the inside
out

a fiery white lioness
a radiant brilliance
a queen branding
dark piercing eyes

black onyx star-eaters
two event horizons
hungry for the light
of the universe

Fan to Sea

eye saw
        dreams fade
            from day
                to night
dear aurora,
        radiant iridescent sea
            swaying to moonlight's silence
                twirling in colors
                    with indigo skies
oh, sylphina symphony—
        innocence's sighs
            dusk's gentle yawn
                singing butterflies
                    into songs
a kind breeze
        breathing softly,
            sweetly into
                an orchestra
                    of air
—exhaled
        lullabies
            longing to be

dawn's
        newborn
            breath

Log # 666

regardless of the language,
there are too many letters
too many meanings

too many ways
to say
the same old things
using a slightly different image—

sigh, exhale
breathe, inhale
breathing, gasping
withering, dying

—oxygen
carbon

both are a breath of life
if you ask the lion
or the flower

why can't I
just be a dandy
                lion?

to be kissed by your lips
a duality in the breeze
and I blow away with the wind
to make your wishes come true

The Feather of Truth

I tried to write you a poem
but didn't compose a single note
left it blank—a sheet without letters
dare I ruin purity with the stain
as if it could carry the weight of love

I folded the edges—words left unsaid
into a paper aeroplane and set them free,
let it fly through the window on the top floor
of my apartment building

I know not where the air carried it
or why it flew so gracefully, likely missing
a heaviness that should have existed

I turned my back as it took off against the wind
heading in the direction of another distant horizon

never to be seen again

Love as Adulation

the acolyte spins—
a wanted divinity
from that
which seeks
to be faithless

drawn in
by the twirling—
illusions of gravity,
a Sufi drowning
zealously in faith

when trumpets beckon,
all shall remain standing
faithfully—
except the dazed

Biblical

I want to write a timeless piece

black lines on white paper?
the contrast is already pretty

just look at the letters,
such sensual shapes
curving into poetry

hands creating
from nothing
eternal treasures

the big bang
in every piece of paper—
you're a god just for trying
existence never made sense
so don't bother explaining

that's madness
you're insane
for thinking
brilliance
is in-
        -sanity

Embers of Babel

scorched Babylon
towers of fire

incandescent gods—
belief in flames

faith ablaze
only ashes remain
in my cremated state

Humanity's First Sin

should one reject the truth
for the sake of love
if the mind is analyzing
every waking breath,
tortured thoughts
in every gasp?

choking on analysis
the results lacking sanity
the steps taken don't quite measure
the distance crossed

should one ache be traded
for another type of hurt?
is the ugliness of truth
really worth hiding?

my mind spins
the questions lingering
in spaces not meant to exist—
or so they say

but here I am again
the same old equations
presented in a slightly
different way

and the sum of shade
still equals a familiar
painful hue

in the end,
it's a marriage
of three ancient letters
w
      h
          y

Cli·ché

paint with words
create an image
the colors of ache,
make them pretty—
vivid yet beautifully subtle

break with style
curve with purpose
it will be timeless,
one meant for the ages

drag a river from the west
make it a neighbor of its east
try to convey a meaning
for meaningless tears

write of silence said aloud,
to talk without speaking
or speak without talking
a clever paradox
almost heard

create tomorrow's clichés today,
recycled from the same old,
same old emotions
so familiar, hello stranger

let readers hang off the edges
end each line with oomph
emphasize, go on, describe
how unbearable relentless
pain really is

but let the reasons remain anonymous
twist the definitions
'til they become synonymous
with isolation

prove worthiness—
let the world know
that the color of blood
is still red

as if that were
ever in question

Carbon is Poison

do you know where great rhythm comes from?
—the way love squeezes a delicate muscle
beating, just trying to find meaning
in senseless breathing

an embrace like a boa constrictor
making red ink from sacred blood

but there's no life
pumping inside—
it's all black and dried
displayed on paper

cliché after cliché—
write me better
shape my worth into
golden letters

you can't embrace my essence
if you never transcend your own
fucked existence

divinity created mercilessly
through the apotheosis of kneeling,
swallowing belief

taking in
pure white faith
a testament to biology
how life first emerged
in salt-tasting waters

legs spread, an ocean of depth
wet from devoted adulation

God is a woman
intimate at night

and a hung devil
in the morning

not just the king
of heaven but also its queen

both lights twinkle
with glimmers of false hope
and the fabricated promise of a new dawn

Questions

humanity died
on the lips of God

the devil knew
when he spoke
and said,

I, a *jinni*, made smokeless fire!
kneel before Adam, the majesty of dirt?

oh almighty, knower of all things,
where is your wisdom tonight?

I will show you the path of humanity
when they wake to dawn,
chasing me like a star
meant to be wished upon

but I grant none except to those
who trade their soul for a moment
to shine beneath the light
of a few forgotten suns

I Let a Fifth in Today

she was on her knees taking me in
it was my first time in someone's mouth

and I stood there watching
admiring how pretty she looked
how her figure made a giant of me

she came looking for love,
some image of it at least,
one I don't quite understand
but the scent—the shape it took,
familiar somehow

I watched
how beautiful, I thought—
thinking about the good of it
for my ego

how tragic, I think now
reflecting on my memories—
wondering why there were four
and none of them aware of any other

her or me
myself or I

Sigmund Freud

it isn't the incestuous connotations
that makes us turn away
it's in the first glimpses of duality
and the truth of their unity

we only see one side
yet can come to know both
how we are broken
and made whole again

it begins with just two
the father and the mother
how we come to know
black and white
through their missing faces
or bright, angry presence

how he leaves
so you come to know
absence

how it lingers—like him
in the cavities of your being

how he stays
and you come to know faith

how it becomes less
with his hands on your face
on your breasts

Baptized in Tears

witness a child
torn from the outside
in

crushed beneath
the weight of her father

God was born from her helpless cries
for a daughter's essence is pure innocence
creating a deity through belief

but the creature
conceived through torture
is corrupted by the conception—
cruelty masquerading
as a merciful Messiah

it just watched
as she was ripped apart
betrayed by faith, by love,
by trust misplaced
in her parents' arms
hands that held her
all wrong

forsaken
by a merciless god
letting night
breathe into dawn
again
      and again
           and again

Faith

to know
and go on
knowing

the sadness
that has painted
so much of my being
is the doorway to love,
the only one I ever found

in the depths of its murky waters,
I've only ever witnessed blurry reflections
but that was always enough
to break the silence

so now I speak slowly,
breathe these breaths

s l o w l y

hoping to find comfort
in the misplaced faith
of today and tomorrow

Feelings

do I describe the room?
the year, the place, the time I'm in?

should I speak of the moment—
the emotions of waving oceans?

every greeting
a tsunami

Georgia

I let her kiss my nose
her breath reeks,
smelling of fish

but I let her do it anyway
I like the way she loves me

her tongue feels like sandpaper
as if she were trying to exfoliate
my skin of its impurities

and Georgia has no clue
that she
                    is a he

a boy named George Banana
yet Mr. Banana wouldn't care
if he's male or female

The Little Ba-na-na
would respond to
any name I call
you see, Georgia
is happy just to have *a home,*
a house built on love with an address
somewhere in the middle *of my heart*

for a winter cat with fur that long
was never meant for the summer heat
found in Las Vegas streets

Oscillation

I watch my cat
staring at a tree
birds singing outside
our second-floor apartment

I reach to pet him
my gorgeous ball of fur

I pause
and reflect
on the image—

the way he's gazing
and patiently waiting
to tear another life apart
feathers, guts, and blood
a vision of horror and gore

conflicted thoughts
stemming from the sight
of an adorable kitten
merely window-watching

Senseless Decades

why curse me
with a thousand memories
yet ask me to wait a lifetime
to kiss the emptiness
found on the lips
of dementia

Poker Face

we've been building homes
on gambles and bets
never the sure thing

we've been wagering our house
to win a second chance at a better life

we've been playing card games
but it's just between the two of us
someone always loses

the dream remains bankrupt
and now we're both drowning in debt
unable to afford a tent, let alone the mansion
you had envisioned

White America

there are Americans
that remind me
I, too, am human

but there are days
where it's so hard
to open my front door

and confront the world
with my color, my brown ethnic skin

Lessons Learned on the Hill

there's hate oozing from the entire world
and if anyone knows it, it's *you*
how it can break people
how it can help them too,
to grow receptive to truth,
to be open to the vulnerability
of not knowing—

exposure to another person
who may seem to write a bit funny
starting from the right side instead of left

اسمي علي

and someone that may pronounce words
from your language in a peculiar way—
churn instead of *turn*

but love comes
in many forms—
a friendship, one that doesn't quite resemble
the one we imagined when we were younger

so let hate be hate—
let those who want to wallow in it do so
and I hope it's in silence,
but if not then only in remarks
and never again shown through violence
and let those of us who know
the wonders of difference
share the virtues of its secrets
with anyone who is willing to listen
because the contrasts in color are beautiful
and that is the most human thing of all—
witnessing iridescence
and embracing the beauty of painted unity

—already forgotten

I say we,
us, and our
quite a bit

as if wanting
to be included
so that I am free
to say these words

if I acknowledge their humanity
then maybe it's okay to share

a reminder of sorts
that I am human too,
as if I somehow forgot
or I am finding myself
in the process of slowly
forgetting

because the world
seems to have—

Earthly Inheritance

it's July 6th, 2019

cellphones light
brighter than the sun
yet we're blind unless
we're looking down

their vibrations rattle our bodies to the core
earthquakes of a different kind
every notification
invoking either dysphoria or elation

but how are we to blame?
for if our gazes are lifted
to meet the world we've inherited,
we are met by the vision
of a planet without hope

Rusted Robot

in a world of shiny sculpted steel
I'm just crumbling rusted metal
obsolete and without purpose
shipped to the scrapyard—

can't make sense
of these senseless
junkyard dreams

Silence

a million
vermillion stories
reside inside

hidden behind
these scorched eyes

sealed and seared

beneath this skin
this dirt, this earth,
this body I call my home

Goodness

I met a black man named James
who wore sunglasses at night

he saved my life
he saw a light
that shined
despite the dark

Ra

darling sun,
won't you please
shine down on me,
caress me in your warmth
illuminate my skies, my seas
and the ground beneath my feet

Pegasus Folds Blank Sheets

finding new purpose
in paper aeroplanes

he turned his back
as he set them loose,
mumbling all the while
how they couldn't anchor
the weight of faith or love

I, too, did not write
my words refused to take flight
to become a winged symphony,
a bird dancing through the clouds
parting overcast skies for a boy
already embraced by light
from a tiny star above

it gave breath
to the breeze,
water to the sea,
moon to the night,
and him to life

Phaethon,
son of Helios,
shaping aura into tender
golden kisses on every part
of the world we call home

Tautology

a morning bird sings
lullabies to the moonlight
and greetings to a sunrise

mountains stand strong,
pillars for the skies to rest upon
when they weep

rainbows and sunshine may fade away
but they always remember to return again
and as such we too must find our place

so

      pause,

           step

                back

                        a n d

                              just

b

   r

      e

         a

           t

              h

                  e

Inner Beauty

some chase beauty
with man's true nature

and some land softly
like a bumblebee
regardless of the radiance
a flower may reflect

seeking only the essence
the nectar to make life's best medicine

for if the core is pure
then the taste, smell,
and goodness

can be revisited
a thousand times over
by a single bee

and a river of honey
will flow eternally

Euphoric Efflorescence

oh, seductive vision of passion
your perfect pink petals
lure me in—

Shangri-La in between
your soft, sensitive thighs

edible and delicious,
always eager to be devoured
blooming when I part my lips,
blossoming in my presence
as if my face were the very sun
and my kiss the quenching drops of rain

nectar so
        {mmm, mmm, mmm}
                        indescribable
I come
bumbling, buzzing,
vibrating with newfound erect elation

my body quakes
in orgasmic sensations
from the taste of a sensual flower's
honey-making sweetness
gently embracing my tongue

No Other

it isn't that you didn't love her
rather, you didn't love her alone
somehow there was another
equally worthy of devotion

in her mind she is autumn
and the other is spring
seasons were never meant
to take place on the same day

we all want to be unique
faithfully believing
in the deification
of our image

and as the Muslims have learned to say,

la illah ila Allah
    there is no other divinity
        but that of the almighty

she too now believes
in a monotheistic view
of her own apotheosis

she alone occupies the throne
a goddess in the kingdom
of eyes that must only see her

Ablaze

what more need I say of us?
you've convinced the world
that the orange hues of fire
are just another shade
of an overarching rainbow
so majestic, so vast, so grand
so many so's
                    so many no's
no,
        enough
                is enough

I asked you to mimic the image
of a smile plastered on the sky
not realizing or maybe forgetting
you're the very devastation
the hurricane of destruction
that had left ashes and ruins
trembling in its wake

if your eyes could cry the truth of you
rain and embers would wash opposite sides

but you're immune to their elements
to what was created inside your vessel

divine is damn right
but so was the devil

Scarlet Horizon

anger
blood boiling
red fire rising
painting the skies
in crimson hues

I am raining
drowning sadness
in acid

embers and ashes
let the color of love
burn away in my hatred

Madness

I didn't ask sanity of the rain
wondering where in the rhythm
I may locate a single drop of reason

I didn't ask for the seasons to change
to replace summer with a cold embrace
let alone to wave farewell to a refreshing spring

I didn't ask you to shred your chest
then hand me the discarded material
asking to make you whole again

but there's no peace
to be made of pieces

and yet you stare horrified
as if I am the cause
of desolation

Obscene Obesity

heavy
fat from anxiety
eating worry
trading sleep
for gluttony

A Letter to a Thousand Faces

somehow, I forgot the language
that used to make your body ache
with ecstasy

now replaced by a longing,
a desire for a ghost of some man
you used to know

because it doesn't quite feel right
in between your legs anymore
I'm fucking you all wrong

and I keep you lingering
with the almost that could have been
instead all I do is thrust my fears,
my worries, my terrors into you
and now that's all you know

I'm sorry I was the hammer
and not the quiet serenity
in a warm cup of tea—
the green of wisdom

instead I was the shaking,
anxious viciousness of black tar,
holding you stubbornly in place,
keeping you wide awake with worry
and repeating the cycle the next morning,
my darkness filling your mouth

I know it wasn't all bad
but nothing stays like fear
nothing soaks in like hurt—
not faith, not peace

I should have been quiet,
learned to love better,

but all I knew was fear
without knowing what I was
afraid of

I became my own horror
in your sunset eyes

and yet you refuse to give us rest,
wanting to see the sunrise reflected
in my lifeless glances

I Hear a Whale's Song

sometimes it's a nightmare

                                    sometimes it's a dream
                                  sometimes it's a comfort

sometimes it's a horror
sometimes it's of you

                                    sometimes it's of me

Static—

I can't dream
if your absence is a nightmare
you're the very breath that I breathe

it would hurt without you
it's even painful just thinking about it

how can you tear me apart,
just shred me to pieces?

knowing I hang onto your every word
as if you're some sort of god
and I'm in desperate need of you,
my savior

I'm just an echo
and you're the very
voice of reason

without you
I am nothing
but white noise

October

I sold my tongue to time—
chose silence as my symphony
spoke sorrow through glances
sadness through gazes

heartbreak
in the dark color
of my eyes

Relative

love
isn't greater
than hate

nor peace
more powerful than war

and good has never overcome evil

but we go on

pretending
        pretending
                pretending

to have the cure—
words worth their weight
in self-absorbed truth

Miscommunication

I could write
to make right

of all that
was left
unsaid

double meanings
and still not one
whole definition

Between the Bloodlines

desolation in silence—
in slow tortured breaths

everyone

> *l*
> *e*
> *a*
> *v*
> *e*
> *s*

yet their fingerprints stay like stains on the heart
and their footprints can be found in every single thought
you follow in their tracks, touching what used to be

they're gone,
you tell yourself

but the feelings
linger on

Clockwork Asylum

:59 ticks
2 breathing its last breath
and fading with time

3 a.m. breathes,
newborn seconds stammering,
entering and leaving—
a house of infinite guests
almost familiar
yet somehow remaining strangers
regardless of their frequent visits

I fear the dark a little less
though shadows still linger
wide awake in the witching hour
shifting between the corners
pursuing me from room to room

my skin rises, hairs follow too
a chill grips me—a cold river roaming
along the curvature of my spine
always keeping me *up*·right
in the middle of the night

awake to insanity, silhouettes dancing—
ethereal creatures wearing the many faces
of mourning

Log #1

how strange to seek such strangeness—
to believe the heart can take residence
in a chest outside its own and yet remain
true to self, to life but not death
                              ....?

but not

what call to the void is this
to see the world
from else's eyes
and in the process
become forgotten to sight

and sight forgets to hum the sounds
that kept dreams of the deep blinded
with the blooming of two irises
the mercy of it—

the madness
of eyes being shut,
open to the world
but closed to seeing

Log #2

I should leave it blank

nothing can come to resemble depth
even between the deepest of oceans

nothing (p r o a
it's just   e s n l)

to be submerged in reflection
rather than drowning in another's essence

so detached from ourselves
yet constantly seeking comfort
in
      an
           other

Insomniac

I feel the quiet
the silent creep
to hush the loud madness
of 32 tortured years

there's been peace
moments of respite
but only echoes,
not completed speech

fragments,
not the whole
of one piece

Just the Echoes Remain

every breath
more tired than the last
though I've danced
with death many times
here I am—still breathing

and breathing
      and breathing
            and breathing

for God?
      for love?
         for me?

I lie awake
      lie awake
lie
      awake

repeating
and choking

on
      and
         on
            and
               on

The Conjuring

we speak of
black and white
as if there's only
dark and light

but to dark
there's also darkness

like memories of green
when only ever witnessed was blue
yet its shade seems so familiar
that they blur into the same image

and lest we forget
        we should not offend
                that great grey abyss
                whose gravity
                is heavier than both

despite its unholy call
we come to know beautifully
the horror of its echoes,
conjured to its door—

just as nothing
is to the void

Naïve

let me tell you a story about a place
where the sun doesn't rise one day
and it doesn't the next
or the day after that

month after month passes by
yet the sun refuses to shine

and those of us living in such a place
now doubt it was ever there
because they've become accustomed
to the cold and the darkness
that now surrounds them

there is another part to this story
where the sun doesn't set

but that too is a sadness
because those living there
think that it will shine forever

when it doesn't
when it couldn't

Twilight in Lions

I learned to let heat
rise out of me
even when set ablaze

I am not a furnace
created to keep cold hands warm
either through touch or presence

a flame needs air
and I refuse to breathe
anything that might become kindling
for the fires meant to be made
within my being

Night and Day

twilight poured
through the gaps
in between the blinds
painting subtle orange hues
on the curtains belonging to
a pair of closed eyes

I turn my back to the window
choosing to sleep and rest further
instead of waking to force the day
before it was ready to start

if I had to describe the feeling,
I don't think I'd have the words
to capture the emotions

but if I had no choice
I'd say it's more like a stream
becoming a river further down
as it trickles into motion
from the warm kisses
placed by golden rays
of the sun

drops of rain once slumbering
huddled together for an entire season
in the shape of snow on the peak of a mountain
now stir, ready to run
springing to begin a marathon
beneath the light of a new dawn

there have been many yesterdays
where life-sustaining waters
rose, swelling with rage
transforming into a flood

devastation brimming on the shores

promising to destroy the surroundings
that could have only existed
on the brink of its presence

tomorrow will come
that much I'm sure
but today is already here

and I need to rebuild a desolated house
back into a vision of home again

The Promise

I feel these words
that stir deep inside me,
they shake my very being
trying to reach the surface

I sway but not to the sounds of music—
no, I move to the hum of my heart
to the melody of my soul

I wonder why
it's always been
that same sad song

of all the visions that haunt me,
growing old alone has to be
the most terrifying

day in and day out
all I can think of
is this person
that I have yet
to meet

I want to wake up to the sounds of a home—
a million noises merging together
into something we call

love

—Your Name

California smile
and sunset eyes

my voice trembling
you're an earthquake
in every breath
I breathe
tonight

mouth curving to the letters,
syllables lingering on the tip of the tongue
and lips parting to moan the true sound
of love—

Naked Art

frozen in suspense
by a girl half my size

she has me pinned against the couch
I move my hands along the sides of her thighs
resting them slightly above her hips

she smiles and lingers on the letter o
before leaning down to kiss me

Atlantis

we were walking home
retreating for the day
from our college town campus
somewhere in Pennsylvania

our hips aligned
we strolled side by side
reflecting on the sight above
beneath a setting evening sun
thinking, talking, laughing aloud

and dusk awoke to share its shade
with countless cumulus clouds
painting the sky as if it were
Claude Monet himself

we spoke of dreams
simple little desires—
kissing in the rain

and out of the blue
it suddenly poured
the weight of an ocean

lightning lit the sky
as you parted your lips
to lock them with mine

One Step at a Time

sometimes you're a serene scene,
a benevolence swaying in the breeze—
a delicate daisy dancing

I just want to sigh,
close my eyes
and smile

why linger in sorrow
when in the presence
of sights this sweet

yes, some flowers hurt to touch
but that doesn't take away
from the happiness found
standing in a garden

so embrace the visions
and the scent of roses
despite the thorns

that may
or may not

exist

Euphoria

in another nameless city
among all the chaos
and the hellish
day to day tasks
I found paradise

waking to a vision
I can only describe
as the true shape
of love—

warmth walking
around our home
wearing sweatpants
and hair tucked
into a ponytail

Someday's Dream

honestly, I just want to be a father,
and for a beautiful baby to smile
at their gorgeous mother—
a child with olive skin
and honey-colored eyes

I want an abode full of joy,
with many years of encouragement
a tiny flashlight to shine on
the little bits of darkness
that creep in unannounced

I want there to be
endless blissful songs
dedicated to random silliness

these are my wants,
seemingly meaningless
yet priceless moments
of eternal happiness

I want a house
to call a home

where fear is a stranger
and comfort is a relative—
family that visits often
and lingers for a time,
but never long enough

Ali Nuri

Heart-Shaped Nostalgia

I say your name in my thoughts
but it just escapes my mouth
as a sound of inexplicable love

mmm

I moan the true shape of you
the letters threatening
to rewrite the core of me
into a word synonymous
with happiness

I miss walking Barcelona streets drunk on mojitos
and the intoxicating swing of your hips

I lost my way following the sensations
the emotions your silhouette stirs inside me,
the way your shadow curves

I'm in awe, witnessing pure ecstasy
I linger, tracing the sight with my gaze
undressing the blissful vision with my mind

you move more than just my being into motion
I move chasing more than another meaningless tail

in flight,
flying high
on your perfume
savoring,
craving

the scent of you
my beautiful wife

About the Author

Ali Nuri was born in Diwaniya, Iraq in 1987. In 1990, Saddam Hussein attacked the city in the middle of the night, forcing thousands of Shi'a to make a painful choice: flee the only home they've ever known or face unspeakable torture. Together the families crossed the desert and awaited the processing of their asylum claims within the confines of a refugee camp located in Saudi Arabia. Subject to unsanitary conditions, thousands of people were crowded into a small enclosure without any facilities to accommodate their basic needs, their dignity, and their humanity. After four years, the family's asylum request was granted and they moved to the U.S., residing in Pennsylvania, Michigan, and Indiana. His family moved from city to city, both nationally and internationally. Being displaced at a young age had left him torn between two cultures that heavily conflicted with each other and feeling as though he didn't belong in his entirety to one or the other. During his teenage years, Ali started writing as a challenge to overcome his dyslexia and struggles with bilingualism, joining supportive online communities to connect with other writers and hone the voice he had spent his childhood silencing. He is now a poet, an author, and an artist. He holds a degree in urban planning and works in the technology industry in Las Vegas, Nevada.

You can connect with me on:
ali-nuri.com
f facebook.com/alinuriofficial
⊙ nomadic_existence

Made in the USA
Lexington, KY
20 September 2019